BEST-EVER
BREAD
COOKBOOK

Consultant Editor:
Valerie Ferguson

southwater

Contents

Introduction

It is difficult to think of a more appetizing aroma than that of baking bread or anything more satisfying than biting into the crisp crust and crumbly inside of a home-made roll. Making bread is a pleasure, too, as you can work off the day's frustrations during the kneading process.

Using yeast as the raising or leavening agent takes time, even with easy-blend dried yeast, but it is not difficult. You can always get on with something else, and for those in a hurry, there are many traditional breads that use faster raising agents.

The range of bread in supermarkets is increasingly extensive and it may seem as if there is little point in home baking. However, it is certainly worth it for special occasions and for making everyday meals a treat. A herb loaf and a fine cheese can turn a snack lunch into a mini-feast. Start the day with home-made croissants dripping with butter and enjoy a reviving slice of fruit loaf with a cup of tea. Make entertaining easy by serving a rich stew with a rustic bread or a spicy curry and hot naan.

"Breaking bread" together is an ancient symbol of friendship and hospitality. The modern equivalent may be to offer it fresh from your own oven.

Ingredients

Above: A range of flours used for bread.

Flour White flour has a high gluten content, absorbs water readily and produces an elastic dough when kneaded. Strong white flour, made from hard wheat with a high proportion of gluten, is specifically for bread making. Wholemeal flour, containing the complete wheat kernel, produces coarser-textured bread with a high fibre content and a stronger flavour. Rye flour is dark and quite dense. It is often mixed with strong wheat flour to give a lighter loaf. Granary flour is a proprietary name given to a mixture of brown and rye flour and malted wheat grain.

Leavening Agents These all work on similar principles. When activated, carbon dioxide is produced and this makes the dough expand, trapping air in tiny pockets throughout. When the bread is baked, the air is locked in, making it light in texture.

Yeast is the traditional leavening agent. Fresh yeast is said to produce the best flavour. It requires warmth to make it work, but over-heating will kill it. Store it in the fridge. Dried yeast is an easily available substitute. It also requires a preliminary mixing with lukewarm liquid. Dough made with fresh or dried yeast requires two sessions of proving (setting aside to increase in bulk). Easy-blend dried yeast can be added directly to the dry ingredients for the dough, which requires only a single proving.

Baking powder is an effective raising agent when added to plain flour. Bicarbonate of soda is activated by acid, such as buttermilk. They both start working immediately they are combined with liquid and the dough does not require proving.

Salt An essential ingredient in yeast breads, salt stops the yeast from working too quickly.

Sweeteners A little sugar is usually added to fresh yeast to give it a good start. It is not needed with easy-blend dried yeast. As sugar slows down the action of yeast, sweet dough may need extra yeast and longer proving.

Honey may also be used in sweet breads. Malt extract, a sugary by-product of barley, has a strong flavour and adds moistness. Molasses or black treacle, by-products of sugar refining, have a strong, smoky, slightly bitter taste.

Liquid Water is the liquid most often used in bread-making, but milk is also popular. It should be lukewarm for yeast dough. Quantities in recipes are for guidance, as flours vary in how much they will absorb.

Flavourings Sweet and savoury flavourings may be incorporated in the dough when it is being kneaded. These include sautéed onions, celery or courgettes, sun-dried tomatoes, fresh or dried herbs, ground spices, cheese, dried fruit, glacé cherries, candied peel and chopped nuts. Be careful when adding ingredients with a high fat content, such as cheese, because too much will spoil the texture of the bread. Nuts, dried fruits, seeds, vegetables and grated cheese may also be used as toppings. Adding oil, butter or margarine to the dough improves

Above: Granary (top), wholemeal and white breads make excellent toast.

the softness of the crumb and delays staleness. Too much, however, impairs the action of the yeast.

Eggs Eggs add flavour and colour and have the benefit of improving the keeping quality of rich breads.

Above: A selection of white breads.

Techniques

Using Fresh Yeast Crumble into a small bowl, add a pinch of sugar and cream the mixture with lukewarm water. Set aside in a warm place for 5–10 minutes, until frothy. Add to the dry ingredients.

Using Dried Yeast Sprinkle on to lukewarm liquid, preferably water, and add a pinch of sugar. Stir and set aside for 10–15 minutes, until frothy. Add to the dry ingredients.

Using Easy-blend Dried Yeast Add straight from the sachet to the dry ingredients. Mix the dough with lukewarm liquid.

Sponging Dissolve the yeast in more lukewarm water than usual, then mix with some of the flour to make a batter. Set aside for a minimum of 20 minutes, until bubbles appear. Mix with the remaining flour.

A Few Simple Rules
- Warm bowls and equipment.
- For lukewarm water (37–43°C/ 98–108°F), mix two parts cold with one part boiling water.
- Knead the dough for at least 10 minutes to stretch the gluten and produce a light-textured loaf.
- Do not leave the dough to prove in a draught.
- Cover the dough while proving to keep it moist.

Adding Fats Add diced butter or margarine to the dry ingredients and rub in with the fingertips until the mixture resembles breadcrumbs. Add oil with the liquid.

Kneading by Hand Turn the dough out on to a lightly floured surface. With floured hands, fold it towards you, pulling and stretching, then push it down firmly with the heel of your hand. Give it a quarter turn and repeat the action for about 10 minutes, until the dough is smooth, elastic and no longer sticky.

Kneading in a Food Processor Do not try to knead more dough than recommended by the manufacturer. If necessary, knead in batches. Fit the dough blade and blend together the dry ingredients. Add the yeast mixture, lukewarm liquid, oil or butter, if using, and process until the mixture comes together. Knead for 1 minute, or according to the manufacturer's instructions. Turn out and knead by hand for 1–2 minutes.

Kneading in a Mixer Mix the dry ingredients. Add the yeast mixture, liquid, oil or butter, if using, and mix slowly with the dough hook until the mixture comes together. Continue for 3–4 minutes, or according to the manufacturer's instructions.

Proving This is the process of setting the dough aside in a warm place to increase in bulk. Keep it moist by covering it with a damp dish towel or lightly oiled plastic wrap. A loaf or rolls on a baking sheet can be slipped inside a plastic bag, ballooned to trap the air. Set aside in a warm place (24–27°C/75–80°F) for an hour or more, until doubled in bulk.

Shaping Rolls To make cottage rolls, shape two-thirds of the dough into rounds the size of golf balls and the remainder into smaller rounds. Make a dent in each large ball and press a small ball on top.

To make knots, roll each dough portion into a fairly thin sausage and knot it like string.

To make twists, twist two strands of dough, dampen the ends and seal.

To make clover-leaf rolls, divide each portion of dough into three equal pieces. Dampen lightly and fit in a bun tin, if liked, pressing lightly to hold.

To make plaits, divide each portion of dough into three equal pieces and roll them into sausages. Dampen them at one end and press together. Plait loosely, dampen the other end and press together.

To make snipped-top rolls, roll each portion of dough into a smooth ball. Snip the top with kitchen scissors.

Glazing Glazing can give an attractive finish and introduces moisture during cooking. Bread may be glazed before, during or just after baking. Glazes include egg yolk, egg white, milk, butter, sugar or salt solutions and olive oil. Take care not to brush glazes up the sides of a tin or drip on a baking sheet, otherwise the bread will stick and crack.

Topping Roll dough in a topping before the second proving or glaze and sprinkle just before baking. Popular toppings include cheese, oats, cracked wheat, sea salt, sunflower, sesame, poppy or caraway seeds, herbs, cornmeal and wheat flakes.

Testing Bread

1 At the end of the cooking time, loosen the edges of the loaf with a palette knife and turn out.

2 Hold the loaf upside down and tap it gently on the base. If it sounds hollow, the bread is ready.

Split Tin

As its name suggests, this popular and homely loaf is so called because of the distinctive centre split.

Makes 1 loaf

INGREDIENTS
500 g/1¼ lb/5 cups unbleached white bread
    flour, plus extra for dusting
10 ml/2 tsp salt
15 g/½ oz fresh yeast
300 ml/½ pint/1¼ cups lukewarm water
60 ml/4 tbsp lukewarm milk

1 Lightly grease a 900 g/2 lb loaf tin. Sift the flour and salt into a bowl and make a well in the centre. Mix the yeast with the lukewarm water. Pour the yeast mixture into the well and mix in a little flour with your fingers. Gradually mix in more of the flour from around the edge of the bowl to form a thick, smooth batter.

2 Sprinkle a little more flour from around the edge of the bowl over the batter and leave in a warm place to sponge. Add the lukewarm milk and remaining flour; mix to a firm dough.

3 Knead on a lightly floured surface for about 10 minutes, until smooth and elastic. Place in a lightly oiled bowl, cover and leave to prove for 1–1¼ hours.

4 Knock back the dough and turn out on to a lightly floured surface. Shape it into a rectangle the length of the tin. Roll up lengthways, tuck the ends under and place seam side down in the tin. Cover and leave to prove for about 20–30 minutes.

5 Using a sharp knife, make a deep slash along the length of the bread; dust with flour. Leave for 15 minutes.

6 Meanwhile, preheat the oven to 230°C/450°F/Gas 8. Bake for 15 minutes, then reduce the oven temperature to 200°C/400°F/Gas 6. Bake for 20–25 minutes more, or until the bread is golden and ready. Turn out on to a wire rack to cool.

COOK'S TIP: Another sure sign that the loaf is ready is that it will have shrunk slightly away from the sides of the tin.

Country Bread

This traditional American loaf, made with a mixture of wholemeal and white flours, not only tastes delicious, but also looks wonderful.

Makes 2 loaves

INGREDIENTS
275 g/10 oz/2½ cups wholemeal flour,
   plus extra for dusting
275 g/10 oz/2½ cups plain flour
115 g/4 oz/1 cup strong
   white flour
20 ml/4 tsp salt
50 g/2 oz/4 tbsp butter,
   at room temperature
475 ml/16 fl oz/2 cups lukewarm milk

FOR THE STARTER
1 sachet easy-blend dried yeast
250 ml/8 fl oz/1 cup
   lukewarm water
115 g/4 oz/1 cup plain flour
1.5 ml/¼ tsp sugar

1 For the starter, stir together the yeast, water, flour and sugar. Cover and leave in a warm place for 2–3 hours or overnight in a cool place.

2 Place the flours, salt and butter in a food processor and process for 1–2 minutes, until just blended. Stir together the milk and starter, then slowly pour into the processor, with the motor running, until the mixture forms a dough. If necessary, add more water. Alternatively, mix the dough by hand. Transfer to a floured surface and knead until smooth and elastic.

3 Place in an ungreased bowl, cover and leave to prove for about 1½ hours.

4 Transfer to a floured surface and knead briefly. Return to the clean bowl and leave to prove for about 1½ hours.

5 Divide the dough in half. Cut off one-third of the dough from each half and shape into balls. Shape the larger remaining portion of each half into balls. Grease a baking sheet.

6 Top each large ball with a small one. Press the centre with the handle of a wooden spoon to secure. Slash the top, cover with a plastic bag and let rise.

7 Preheat the oven to 200°C/400°F/ Gas 6. Bake the dough, sprinkled with wholemeal flour, for 45–50 minutes, until browned. Cool on a rack.

Granary Cob

You can make this loaf plain, with a slash across the top for a Danish cob or with a cross cut in the top for a Coburg cob.

Makes 1 loaf

INGREDIENTS
450 g/1 lb/4 cups Granary flour
10 ml/2 tsp salt
15 g/½ oz fresh yeast
300 ml/½ pint/1¼ cups lukewarm water
    or milk and water mixed

FOR THE TOPPING
30 ml/2 tbsp water
2.5 ml/½ tsp salt
wheat flakes or cracked wheat,
    to sprinkle

1 Lightly flour a baking sheet. Sift the flour and salt into a bowl and make a well in the centre. Place in a very low oven for 5 minutes to warm.

2 Mix the yeast with a little of the lukewarm water or milk mixture then blend in the rest. Add the yeast mixture to the centre of the warmed Granary flour and mix well to form a dough.

3 Turn the dough out on to a lightly floured surface and knead for about 10 minutes, until smooth and elastic. Place in a lightly oiled bowl, cover and leave to prove for about 1¼ hours.

4 Turn the dough out on to a lightly floured surface and knock back. Knead for 2–3 minutes, then roll into a ball. Place in the centre of the prepared baking sheet. Cover with an inverted bowl and leave to prove again for 30–45 minutes.

5 For the topping, mix the water and salt and brush over the bread. Sprinkle the surface with wheat flakes or cracked wheat. Preheat the oven to 230°C/450°F/Gas 8.

6 Bake the Granary loaf for 15 minutes, then reduce the oven temperature to 200°C/400°F/Gas 6 and bake for 20 minutes more, or until the loaf is ready. Leave to cool on a wire rack.

Wholemeal Bread

The temptation to cut a slice of this bread while it is still warm and eat it smothered in melting butter is almost irresistible.

Makes 4 round or
2 tin-shaped loaves

INGREDIENTS
20 g/¾ oz fresh yeast
300 ml/½ pint/1¼ cups lukewarm milk
5 ml/1 tsp caster sugar
225 g/8 oz/1½ cups strong wholemeal
    flour, sifted
225 g/8 oz/2 cups strong white flour, sifted
5 ml/1 tsp salt
50 g/2 oz/4 tbsp butter, chilled and cubed
1 egg, lightly beaten
30 ml/2 tbsp mixed seeds, to sprinkle

1 Dissolve the yeast with a little of the milk and the sugar to make a paste. Place both flours plus any bran and the salt in a bowl. Rub in the butter until the mixture resembles breadcrumbs.

2 Add the yeast mixture, remaining milk and egg. Mix to a soft dough. Knead for 15 minutes on a floured board. Put into a lightly greased bowl, cover and let prove for about 1 hour.

3 Knock back the dough and knead it for a further 10 minutes on a lightly floured surface. Preheat the oven to 200°C/400°F/Gas 6.

4 Round loaves: divide the dough into four. Shape into flattish rounds and prove on a floured baking sheet for 15 minutes. Sprinkle with seeds. Bake for about 20 minutes until golden. Cool on wire racks. Tin-shaped loaves: put the knocked-back dough into two greased loaf tins, prove for 45 minutes and bake for about 45 minutes.

Soda Bread

This takes only a few minutes to make and needs no proving. Eat it while still warm from the oven.

Makes 1 loaf

INGREDIENTS
450 g/1 lb/4 cups plain flour
5 ml/1 tsp salt
5 ml/1 tsp bicarbonate
of soda
5 ml/1 tsp cream of tartar
350 ml/12 fl oz/1½ cups
buttermilk

1 Preheat the oven to 220°C/425°F/ Gas 7. Flour a baking sheet. Sift all the dry ingredients into a mixing bowl and make a well in the centre.

2 Add the buttermilk and mix quickly to a soft dough. Turn on to a floured surface and knead very briefly and lightly. (The aim is just to get rid of the largest cracks, as the dough will become tough if it is handled for too long.)

3 Shape the loaf into a round about 18 cm/7 in in diameter and place on the baking sheet. Cut a deep cross on the top of the loaf and sprinkle with a little flour. Bake for 25–30 minutes, then transfer to a wire rack to cool.

Sourdough Rye Bread

Packed with flavour, this substantial rustic bread originated in Germany, but is now enjoyed in many countries.

Makes 2 loaves

INGREDIENTS
10 ml/2 tsp easy-blend dried yeast
120 ml/4 fl oz/½ cup lukewarm water
25 g/1 oz/2 tbsp butter, melted
15 ml/1 tbsp salt
115 g/4 oz/1 cup wholemeal flour
400–450 g/14 oz–1 lb/3½–4 cups
    plain flour
1 egg mixed with 15 ml/1 tbsp water,
    for glazing

FOR THE STARTER
1 sachet easy-blend dried yeast
350 ml/12 fl oz/1½ cups lukewarm water
45 ml/3 tbsp treacle or molasses
30 ml/2 tbsp caraway seeds
275 g/10 oz/2½ cups rye flour

1 For the starter, stir together the yeast and lukewarm water and leave for 15 minutes to dissolve. Stir in the treacle or molasses, caraway seeds and rye flour. Cover and leave in a warm place for 2–3 days.

2 In a large bowl, stir together the yeast and lukewarm water and leave the mixture for 10 minutes. Stir in the melted butter, salt, wholemeal flour and 400 g/14 oz/3½ cups of the plain flour.

3 Make a well in the centre and pour in the starter. Stir the mixture to make a rough dough, adding extra flour if the mixture is too wet, then transfer it to a floured surface and knead until it is smooth and elastic. Return the dough to the bowl, cover and leave to prove for about 2 hours.

4 Grease a large baking sheet. Knock back the dough and knead briefly. Cut the dough in half and form each half into a log-shaped loaf.

COOK'S TIP: If the tops of the loaves start to brown too quickly, protect them with a sheet of foil for the rest of the cooking time.

5 Place the loaves on the baking sheet and score the tops with a sharp knife. Cover and leave to prove for about 50 minutes. Preheat the oven to 190°C/375°F/Gas 5.

6 Brush the loaves with the glaze. Bake for 50–55 minutes, until ready. Cool on a rack.

French Bread

This is a bread that must be eaten on the day it is made – preferably as soon as it has cooled from the oven.

Makes 2 loaves

INGREDIENTS
1 sachet easy-blend dried yeast
475 ml/16 fl oz/2 cups
    lukewarm water
15 ml/1 tbsp salt
675–900 g/1½–2 lb/6–8 cups
    plain flour
cornmeal, to sprinkle

1 Combine the yeast and water, stir, and leave for 15 minutes to dissolve. Stir in the salt.

2 Add the flour, 115 g/4 oz/1 cup at a time. Beat in with a wooden spoon, adding just enough flour to obtain a smooth dough. Alternatively, you can use an electric mixer with a dough hook attachment.

3 Transfer the dough to a floured surface and knead until it is smooth and elastic.

4 Shape into a ball, place in a greased bowl and cover. Leave to prove for 2–4 hours.

> COOK'S TIP: The thin French stick is known as a baguette, meaning a "wand", while a thicker, but still long, loaf is called "pain".

5 Transfer to a lightly-floured board and shape into two long loaves. Place on a baking sheet sprinkled with cornmeal. Leave the loaves to prove for 5 minutes.

6 Score the tops of the loaves with a very sharp knife in several places. Brush with water and place in a cold oven. Set a pan of boiling water on the bottom of the oven and set the oven to 200°C/400°F/Gas 6. Bake for about 40 minutes, until crusty and golden. Cool on a rack.

Ciabatta

This irregular-shaped Italian bread is made with a very wet dough flavoured with olive oil.

Makes 3 loaves

INGREDIENTS
15 g/½ oz fresh yeast
400 ml/14 fl oz/1⅔ cups
    lukewarm water
60 ml/4 tbsp lukewarm milk
500 g/1¼ lb/5 cups unbleached
    white bread flour
10 ml/2 tsp salt
45 ml/3 tbsp extra virgin
    olive oil

FOR THE STARTER
10 g/¼ oz fresh yeast
175–200 ml/6–7 fl oz/¾–scant 1 cup
    lukewarm water
350 g/12 oz/3 cups unbleached plain flour,
    plus extra, for dusting

1 Cream the fresh yeast for the starter with a little of the lukewarm water. Sift the plain flour into a large bowl. Gradually mix in the yeast mixture and sufficient of the remaining water to form a firm dough.

2 Turn out the starter dough on to a lightly floured surface and knead for about 5 minutes, until smooth and elastic. Return to the bowl, cover and leave to prove for 12–15 hours.

3 Sprinkle three baking sheets with flour. Mix the yeast for the dough with a little of the water until creamy, then mix in the remainder. Add the yeast mixture to the starter dough and gradually mix in.

4 Beat in the milk with a wooden spoon. Using your hand, gradually beat in the flour, lifting the dough as you mix. This will take 15 minutes or more and form a very wet mix, impossible to knead on a work surface. Beat in the salt and olive oil. Cover and leave to prove for 1½–2 hours.

5 Using a spoon, carefully tip one-third of the dough at a time on to the prepared baking sheets, trying to avoid knocking it back in the process.

6 Using floured hands, shape into rough loaf shapes, about 2.5 cm/1 in thick. Flatten slightly with splayed fingers. Sprinkle with flour and leave to prove for 30 minutes. Preheat the oven to 220°C/425°F/Gas 7. Bake for 25–30 minutes, or until golden and ready. Cool on a wire rack.

VARIATION: To make tomato-flavoured ciabatta, add 115 g/4 oz/ 1 cup chopped, drained sun-dried tomatoes in olive oil with the olive oil in step 4.

Dill Bread

This would make an excellent accompaniment to serve with a fish soup and also goes well with cheese.

Makes 2 loaves

INGREDIENTS
20 ml/4 tsp easy-blend dried yeast
475 ml/16 fl oz/2 cups
    lukewarm water
30 ml/2 tbsp sugar
850 g/1 lb 14 oz/7½ cups
    plain flour
½ onion, chopped
60 ml/4 tbsp vegetable oil
1 large bunch fresh dill,
    finely chopped
2 eggs, lightly beaten
115 g/4 oz/½ cup cottage cheese
20 ml/4 tsp salt
milk, for glazing

3 Cook the onion in 15 ml/1 tbsp of the oil in a frying pan until soft. Set aside to cool, then stir into the yeast mixture. Stir the dill, eggs, cottage cheese, salt and remaining oil into the yeast mixture. Gradually add the remaining flour until too stiff to stir.

1 Mix together the yeast, water and sugar in a large bowl and leave for 15 minutes to dissolve.

2 Stir in 350 g/12 oz/3 cups of the flour. Cover and leave to prove for 45 minutes.

4 Transfer to a floured surface and knead until smooth and elastic. Place in a bowl, cover and leave to prove for 1–1½ hours.

VARIATION: Try substituting other fresh herbs, such as thyme, for the dill in this recipe.

5 Grease a large baking sheet. Cut the dough in half and shape into two rounds. Leave to prove for 30 minutes.

6 Preheat the oven to 190°C/375°F/ Gas 5. Score the tops, brush with the milk, and bake for about 50 minutes, until browned and ready. Cool on a wire rack.

Spiral Herb Bread

Serve these attractive slices of flavoured bread with a creamy cheese, such as Camembert or dolcelatte.

Makes 2 loaves

INGREDIENTS
2 sachets easy-blend dried yeast
600 ml/1 pint/2½ cups
    lukewarm water
350 g/12 oz/3 cups plain flour
350 g/12 oz/3 cups wholemeal flour
15 ml/1 tbsp salt
25 g/1 oz/2 tbsp butter
1 large bunch fresh parsley,
    finely chopped
1 bunch spring onions,
    finely chopped
1 garlic clove, finely chopped
1 egg, lightly beaten
milk, for glazing
salt and freshly ground
    black pepper

1 Combine the yeast and 60 ml/
4 tbsp of the water, stir and leave for
15 minutes to dissolve.

2 Combine the flours and salt in a
large bowl. Make a well in the centre
and pour in the yeast mixture and the
remaining water. Mix together to
make a rough dough.

3 Transfer the dough to a floured
surface and knead until smooth and
elastic. Return to the bowl, cover and
leave to prove for about 2 hours.

4 Meanwhile, combine the butter,
parsley, spring onions and garlic in a
large frying pan. Cook over a low
heat, stirring, until softened. Season
with salt and pepper and set aside.

5 Grease two 25 x 13 cm/10 x 5 in
loaf tins. Cut the dough in half, then
roll each half into a rectangle about
35 x 23 cm/14 x 9 in. Brush both
with the beaten egg. Divide the herb
mixture between the two, spreading
just up to the edges.

6 Roll up to enclose the filling and pinch the short ends to seal. Place in the tins, seam side down. Cover and leave to prove.

7 Preheat the oven to 190°C/375°F/ Gas 5. Brush with milk and bake for about 55 minutes, until ready. Cool on a wire rack.

Cheese & Courgette Cluster

This unusual bread owes its moistness to grated courgettes and its depth of flavour to freshly grated Parmesan cheese.

Serves 8

INGREDIENTS
4 courgettes, coarsely grated
675 g/1½ lb/6 cups strong white bread flour
2 sachets easy-blend dried yeast
50 g/2 oz/⅔ cup freshly grated
    Parmesan cheese
30 ml/2 tbsp olive oil
milk, to glaze
poppy seeds or sesame seeds,
    to sprinkle
salt and freshly ground black pepper

3 Gather the dough together with your hand, then turn it out on to a lightly floured surface. Knead it for 5–10 minutes, or until it is smooth and elastic. Return to the cleaned bowl, cover and leave to prove for about 1½ hours.

4 Knock back the dough and knead again. Divide it into eight pieces and roll into smooth balls using the palms of your hands.

1 Put the courgettes into a colander and sprinkle with salt. Stand in a sink for about 20 minutes to drain the juices, then rinse thoroughly. Drain and pat dry with kitchen paper.

2 Mix the flour with the yeast, Parmesan and 2.5 ml/½ tsp salt. Add pepper to taste. Stir in the oil and courgettes, then add enough lukewarm water to make a firm, but still soft dough (start with about 45 ml/3 tbsp).

5 Lightly grease a deep 23 cm/9 in cake tin. Fit the balls into the tin, arranging them around the outside with the last one in the centre.

6 Glaze the loaf with a little milk and sprinkle over poppy or sesame seeds. Cover and leave to prove until the balls of dough have doubled in size.

7 Meanwhile, preheat the oven to 200°C/400°F/Gas 6. Bake the loaf for 35–45 minutes, until it is golden brown and ready. Cool on a wire rack.

Sun-dried Tomato Bread

No Italian meal is ever served without bread. This flavourful recipe comes from the south, where the tomatoes are genuinely sun-dried.

Makes 4 loaves

INGREDIENTS
675 g/1½ lb/6 cups strong
    plain flour
10 ml/2 tsp salt
25 g/1 oz/2 tbsp caster sugar
25 g/1 oz fresh yeast
400–475 ml/14–16 fl oz/1⅔–2 cups
    lukewarm milk
15 ml/1 tbsp tomato purée
75 ml/5 tbsp oil from the jar of
    sun-dried tomatoes
75 ml/5 tbsp extra virgin
    olive oil
75 g/3 oz/¾ cup drained sun-dried
    tomatoes, chopped
1 large onion, chopped

1 Sift the flour, salt and sugar into a bowl and make a well in the centre. Crumble the yeast, mix with 150 ml/ ¼ pint/⅔ cup of the milk and add to the flour.

2 Mix the tomato purée into the remaining milk, until evenly blended, then add to the flour with the tomato oil and olive oil.

COOK'S TIP: Use a pair of sharp kitchen scissors to cut up the sun-dried tomatoes.

3 Gradually mix the flour into the liquid ingredients to make a dough. Turn out on to a floured surface and knead for about 10 minutes, until smooth and elastic. Return to the clean bowl, cover and leave to prove for about 2 hours.

4 Knock back the dough and add the tomatoes and onion. Knead until evenly distributed through the dough. Shape into four rounds and place on a greased baking sheet. Cover and leave to prove for about 45 minutes. Preheat the oven to 190°C/375°F/Gas 5. Bake for 45 minutes, or until ready. Cool on a wire rack.

Polenta & Pepper Bread

Full of Mediterranean flavour, this satisfying, sunshine-coloured bread is
best eaten while still warm, drizzled with olive oil and served with soup.

Makes 2 loaves

INGREDIENTS
175 g/6 oz/1½ cups polenta
5 ml/1 tsp salt
350 g/12 oz/3 cups unbleached strong plain
    flour, plus extra for dusting
5 ml/1 tsp sugar
1 sachet easy-blend dried yeast
1 red pepper, roasted,
    peeled and diced
300 ml/½ pint/1¼ cups lukewarm water
15 ml/1 tbsp olive oil

1 Mix together the polenta, salt, flour,
sugar and yeast in a large bowl. Stir in
the diced red pepper until it is evenly
distributed throughout the mixture,
then make a well in the centre. Grease
two loaf tins.

COOK'S TIP: Roast the pepper in
the oven or under a grill until
charred, then place in a plastic bag
and leave until cool enough to peel.

2 Add the lukewarm water and the
oil and mix to a soft dough. Knead for
10 minutes, until smooth and elastic.
Place in an oiled bowl, cover and leave
to prove for 1 hour.

3 Knock back the dough, knead
lightly, then divide in two. Shape each
piece into an oblong and place in the
tins. Cover and leave to prove for
45 minutes. Preheat the oven to
220°C/425°F/Gas 7.

4 Bake the bread for 30 minutes,
until it is golden and sounds hollow
when tapped on the base. Allow to
cool on a wire rack.

Malt Loaf

This is a rich and sticky loaf. If it lasts long enough to go stale, try toasting it for a delicious tea-time treat.

Makes 1 loaf

INGREDIENTS
150 ml/¼ pint/⅔ cup lukewarm milk
5 ml/1 tsp dried yeast
pinch of caster sugar
350 g/12 oz/3 cups plain flour
1.5 ml/¼ tsp salt
30 ml/2 tbsp light
  muscovado sugar
175 g/6 oz/generous
  1 cup sultanas
15 ml/1 tbsp sunflower oil
45 ml/3 tbsp malt extract

FOR THE GLAZE
30 ml/2 tbsp caster sugar
30 ml/2 tbsp water

1 Place the milk in a bowl. Sprinkle the yeast on top and add the sugar. Leave for 30 minutes, until frothy. Sift the flour and salt into a mixing bowl, stir in the muscovado sugar and sultanas, and make a well in the centre.

2 Add the yeast mixture together with the oil and the malt extract. Gradually incorporate the flour from the sides and mix to a soft dough, adding a little extra milk if necessary to achieve the right consistency.

3 Turn on to a floured surface and knead for about 5 minutes, until smooth and elastic. Grease a 450 g/ 1 lb loaf tin.

4 Shape the dough and place it in the prepared tin. Cover and leave to prove for 1–2 hours. Preheat the oven to 190°C/375°F/Gas 5.

5 Bake the loaf for 30–35 minutes, until golden and ready. Meanwhile, prepare the glaze by dissolving the sugar in the water in a small pan. Bring to the boil, stirring, then lower the heat and simmer for 1 minute. Place the loaf on a wire rack and brush with the glaze while still hot. Leave the loaf to cool before serving.

VARIATION: To make buns, divide the dough into ten pieces, shape into rounds, leave to rise, then bake for about 15–20 minutes. Brush with the glaze while still hot.

Banana & Cardamom Bread

The combination of banana and cardamom is delicious in this soft-textured moist loaf. It is perfect for tea time, served with butter and jam.

Makes 1 loaf

INGREDIENTS
150 ml/¼ pint/⅔ cup warm water
5 ml/1 tsp dried yeast
pinch of sugar
10 cardamom pods
400 g/14 oz/3½ cups strong
   white flour
5 ml/1 tsp salt
30 ml/2 tbsp malt extract
2 ripe bananas, mashed
5 ml/1 tsp sesame seeds, to sprinkle

1 Put the water in a small bowl. Sprinkle the yeast on top, add the sugar and mix thoroughly. Leave for 10 minutes. Meanwhile, split the cardamom pods and remove the seeds. Chop the seeds finely.

2 Sift the flour and salt into a mixing bowl and make a well in the centre. Add the yeast mixture with the malt extract, chopped cardamom seeds and mashed bananas.

3 Gradually incorporate the flour and mix to a soft dough, adding a little extra water if necessary. Turn the dough on to a floured surface and knead for about 5 minutes, until smooth and elastic. Return to the clean bowl, cover and leave to prove for about 2 hours.

4 Grease a baking sheet. Turn the dough on to a floured surface, knead briefly, then shape into a plait. Place the plait on the baking sheet, cover and leave to prove. Preheat the oven to 220°C/425°F/Gas 7.

5 Brush the plait lightly with water and sprinkle with the sesame seeds. Bake for 10 minutes, then lower the oven temperature to 200°C/400°F/ Gas 6. Cook for 15 minutes more, or until the loaf is ready. Allow to cool on a wire rack.

Sultana & Walnut Bread

This bread is delicious with savoury or sweet toppings. Try salami, cheese and salad for lunch or jam for breakfast.

Makes 1 loaf

INGREDIENTS

300 g/11 oz/2¾ cups strong plain flour
2.5 ml/½ tsp salt
15 g/½ oz/1 tbsp butter
7.5 ml/1½ tsp easy-blend
   dried yeast
175 ml/6 fl oz/¾ cup lukewarm water
115 g/4 oz/scant 1 cup sultanas
75 g/3 oz/½ cup walnuts,
   roughly chopped
melted butter, for brushing

1 Sift the flour and salt into a bowl, cut in the butter with a knife, then stir in the yeast.

2 Gradually add the lukewarm water, stirring with a spoon at first, then gathering the dough together with your hands.

3 Turn the dough out on to a floured surface. Knead for about 10 minutes, until smooth and elastic.

4 Knead the sultanas and walnuts into the dough until they are evenly distributed. Shape into a rough oval shape, place on a lightly oiled baking sheet, cover and leave to prove for 1–2 hours. Preheat the oven to 220°C/425°F/Gas 7.

5 Uncover the loaf and bake for 10 minutes, then reduce the oven temperature to 190°C/375°F/Gas 5. Bake for a further 20–25 minutes.

6 Transfer the loaf to a wire rack, brush with the melted butter and cover with a dish towel. Allow the loaf to cool before slicing.

Barm Brack

It used to be traditional to bake a wedding ring in this Irish Hallowe'en bread as a marriage charm.

Makes 1 loaf

INGREDIENTS
675 g/1½ lb/6 cups plain flour
2.5 ml/½ tsp mixed spice
5 ml/1 tsp salt
1 sachet easy-blend
   dried yeast
50 g/2 oz/¼ cup caster sugar
300 ml/½ pint/1¼ cups
   lukewarm milk
150 ml/¼ pint/⅔ cup
   lukewarm water
50 g/2 oz/4 tbsp butter, softened
225 g/8 oz/1⅓ cups sultanas
50 g/2 oz/⅓ cup currants
50 g/2 oz/⅓ cup chopped
   mixed peel
milk, for glazing

1 Sift the plain flour, mixed spice and salt into a large bowl. Stir in the dried yeast and 15 ml/1 tbsp of the caster sugar. Make a well in the centre and pour in the lukewarm milk and water.

2 Mix well, gradually incorporating the dry ingredients to make a sticky dough. Place on a lightly floured board and knead the dough until smooth and elastic. Put into a clean bowl. Cover and leave to prove for about 1 hour.

3 Knead the dough lightly on a floured surface. Add the remaining ingredients, apart from the milk for glazing, and work them in. Return the dough to the bowl, cover and leave to prove for 30 minutes.

4 Grease a 23 cm/9 in round cake tin. Pat the dough to a neat round and fit it in the tin. Cover and leave to prove for about 45 minutes.

5 Preheat the oven to 200°C/400°F/ Gas 6. Brush the loaf lightly with milk and bake for 15 minutes. Cover the loaf with foil, reduce the oven temperature to 180°C/350°F/Gas 4 and bake for 45 minutes more, or until golden and ready. Cool on a wire rack.

Panettone

This classic bread can be found throughout Italy around Christmas. It is surprisingly light, even though it is rich with butter and dried fruit.

Makes 1 loaf

INGREDIENTS
400 g/14 oz/3½ cups unbleached white
    bread flour
2.5 ml/½ tsp salt
15 g/½ oz fresh yeast
120 ml/4 fl oz/½ cup lukewarm milk
2 eggs
2 egg yolks
75 g/3 oz/6 tbsp caster sugar
150 g/5 oz/⅔ cup butter, softened
115 g/4 oz/⅔ cup mixed
    chopped peel
75 g/3 oz/½ cup raisins
melted butter, for brushing

1 Using a double layer of greaseproof paper, line and butter a 20 cm/8 in wide/15 cm/6 in deep cake tin or soufflé dish. Finish the paper 7.5 cm/3 in above the top of the tin.

2 Sift the flour and salt into a large bowl. Make a well in the centre. Cream the yeast with 60 ml/4 tbsp of the milk, then mix in the remainder.

3 Pour the yeast mixture into the centre of the flour, add the whole eggs and mix in sufficient flour to make a thick batter. Sprinkle a little of the remaining flour over the top and leave the batter to sponge, in a warm place, for 30 minutes.

4 Add the egg yolks and sugar and mix to a soft dough. Work in the softened butter, then turn out on to a lightly floured surface and knead for 5 minutes, until smooth and elastic. Place in a lightly oiled bowl, cover and leave to prove for 1½–2 hours.

5 Knock back the dough and turn out on to a lightly floured surface. Gently knead in the peel and raisins. Shape into a ball and place in the prepared tin. Cover and leave to prove for about 1 hour.

6 Meanwhile, preheat the oven to 190°C/375°F/Gas 5. Brush the surface with melted butter, and cut a cross in the top using a sharp knife. Bake for 20 minutes, then reduce the oven temperature to 180°C/350°F/Gas 4. Brush the top with butter again and bake for a further 25–30 minutes, or until golden.

7 Allow the Panettone to cool in the tin for 5–10 minutes, then turn it out on to a wire rack to cool.

COOK'S TIP: Once the dough has been enriched with butter, do not prove in too warm a place or the loaf will become greasy.

Pitta Bread

These Turkish breads are a firm favourite in both the eastern Mediterranean and the Middle East, and have crossed to England and the USA. Try serving them with homemade hummus.

Makes 6 pitta breads

INGREDIENTS
225 g/8 oz/2 cups unbleached white
    bread flour
5 ml/1 tsp salt
15 g/½ oz fresh yeast
140 ml/scant ¼ pint/scant ⅔ cup
    lukewarm water
10 ml/2 tsp extra virgin
    olive oil

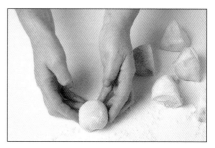

3 Knock back the dough. On a lightly floured surface, divide it into six equal pieces and shape into balls. Cover and let rest for 5 minutes.

1 Sift the flour and salt into a large bowl. Mix the yeast with the water until dissolved, then stir in the olive oil and pour into the bowl containing the flour. Gradually beat the flour into the yeast mixture, then knead the mixture to make a soft dough.

2 Turn out on to a lightly floured surface and knead for 5 minutes, until smooth and elastic. Place in a large clean bowl, cover and leave to prove for about 1 hour.

4 Roll out each ball of dough to an oval about 5 mm/¼ in thick and 15 cm/6 in long. Place on a floured dish towel and cover. Leave to prove for about 20–30 minutes. Meanwhile, preheat the oven to 230°C/450°F/ Gas 8. Place three baking sheets in the oven to heat at the same time.

5 Place two pitta breads on each heated baking sheet and bake for 4–6 minutes, or until puffed up; they do not need to brown. Cook the pitta bread in batches if preferred.

6 Transfer the pittas to a wire rack to cool until warm, then cover with a dish towel to keep them soft.

VARIATIONS: To make wholemeal pitta breads, replace half the white bread flour with wholemeal bread flour. You can also make smaller, round pitta breads about 10 cm/4 in diameter to serve as snack breads.

Naan

Traditionally cooked in a very hot clay oven known as a tandoor, naan are usually eaten with dry meat or vegetable dishes.

Makes 4 naan

INGREDIENTS
225 g/8 oz/2 cups unbleached white
    bread flour
2.5 ml/½ tsp salt
15 g/½ oz fresh yeast
60 ml/4 tbsp lukewarm milk
15 ml/1 tbsp vegetable oil
30 ml/2 tbsp natural yogurt
1 egg
30–45 ml/2–3 tbsp melted ghee or butter,
    for brushing

1 Sift the flour and salt into a bowl. In a smaller bowl, cream the yeast with the milk. Set aside for 15 minutes.

2 Add the yeast mixture, oil, yogurt and egg to the flour and mix to a soft dough. Turn out the dough on to a lightly floured surface and knead for about 10 minutes, until smooth and elastic. Place the dough in a lightly oiled bowl, cover and leave to prove for 45 minutes.

VARIATION: For spicy naan, add 5 ml/1 tsp each ground coriander and ground cumin with the flour in step 1. For extra hot naan, add 2.5–5 ml/½–1 tsp chilli powder at the same time.

3 Preheat the oven to its highest setting, at least 230°C/450°F/Gas 8. Place two heavy baking sheets in the oven to heat.

4 Turn the dough out on to a lightly floured surface and knock back. Divide into four equal pieces and shape into balls. Cover three of the balls of dough with oiled clear film and roll out the fourth into a teardrop shape about 23 cm/9 in long, 13 cm/5 in wide and 5–8 mm/¼–⅓ in thick.

5 Preheat the grill to its highest setting. Meanwhile, place the rolled naan on a hot baking sheet and bake for 3–4 minutes, or until puffed up.

6 Remove the naan from the oven and place under the hot grill for a few seconds, or until the top browns slightly. Wrap in a dish towel to keep warm while rolling out and cooking the remaining naan. Brush with melted ghee or butter and serve warm.

Rosemary & Rock Salt Focaccia

This popular Italian bread is enriched with olive oil and flavoured with rosemary, garlic and black olives.

Makes 1 loaf

INGREDIENTS
225 g/8 oz/2 cups unbleached plain
   flour, sifted
2.5 ml/½ tsp salt
1 sachet easy-blend dried yeast
4 garlic cloves, finely chopped
2 fresh sprigs of rosemary, leaves removed
   and chopped
10 black olives, stoned and roughly
   chopped (optional)
15 ml/1 tbsp olive oil
150 ml/¼ pint/⅔ cup lukewarm water

FOR THE TOPPING
90 ml/6 tbsp olive oil
10 ml/2 tsp rock salt
1 fresh sprig of rosemary, leaves removed

1 Mix together the flour, salt, yeast, garlic, rosemary and olives, if using, in a large bowl. Make a well in the centre and add the olive oil and water. Mix thoroughly to form a soft dough.

VARIATION: To make saffron focaccia, add a few strands of saffron to the warm water and leave to stand for 5 minutes before adding to the flour. Alternatively, add a pinch of saffron powder to the flour.

2 Turn out the dough on to a lightly floured work surface and knead for 10–15 minutes. Put the dough in an oiled bowl and cover. Leave to prove for 45 minutes.

3 Turn out the dough and knead lightly again. Roll out to an oval shape, about 1 cm/½ in thick.

4 Place the dough on a greased baking sheet, cover and leave to prove for 25–30 minutes.

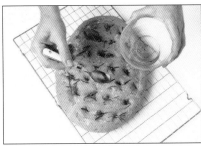

5 Preheat the oven to 200°C/400°F/ Gas 6. Make indentations with your fingertips all over the top of the bread. Drizzle two-thirds of the olive oil over the top, then sprinkle with the rock salt and rosemary. Bake for 25 minutes, until golden and ready. Transfer to a wire rack and spoon the remaining olive oil over the top.

Bread Sticks

Crisp little sticks of bread coated in sesame seeds are the perfect accompaniment to a cold starter.

Makes 18–20 sticks

INGREDIENTS
1 sachet easy-blend dried yeast
300 ml/½ pint/1¼ cups
    lukewarm water
350 g/12 oz/3 cups plain flour
10 ml/2 tsp salt
5 ml/1 tsp sugar
30 ml/2 tbsp olive oil
225 g/8 oz/1 cup
    sesame seeds
1 egg, beaten, for glazing
coarse salt, for sprinkling

1 Combine the yeast and water, stir, and leave for 15 minutes to dissolve. Place the flour, salt, sugar and olive oil in a food processor.

2 With the motor running, slowly pour in the yeast mixture and process until the dough forms a ball. If sticky, add more flour; if dry, add more water.

3 Transfer to a floured surface and knead until smooth and elastic. Place in a bowl, cover and leave to prove for 45 minutes.

4 Lightly toast the sesame seeds in a frying pan. Grease two baking sheets.

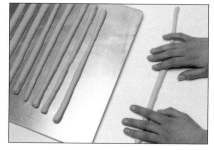

5 Roll small handfuls of dough into cylinders, about 30 cm/12 in long. Place on the baking sheets.

VARIATION: If preferred, use other seeds, such as poppy or caraway or, for plain bread sticks, omit the seeds and salt.

6 Brush with egg glaze, sprinkle with the sesame seeds, then sprinkle over some coarse salt. Leave to prove, uncovered, for about 20 minutes. Preheat the oven to 200°C/400°F/ Gas 6. Bake for about 15 minutes, until golden. Turn off the heat but leave the bread sticks in the oven for 5 minutes more. Serve warm or cool.

Buttery Poppy Seed Knots

These appetizing and professional-looking poppy seed rolls are actually very easy to make.

Makes 12

INGREDIENTS
300 ml/½ pint/1¼ cups lukewarm milk
50 g/2 oz/4 tbsp butter,
    at room temperature
5 ml/1 tsp sugar
10 ml/2 tsp easy-blend dried yeast
1 egg yolk
10 ml/2 tsp salt
400–450 g/14 oz–1 lb/3½–4 cups
    plain flour
1 egg beaten with 10 ml/2 tsp water,
    for glazing
poppy seeds, for sprinkling

1 In a large bowl, stir together the milk, butter, sugar and yeast. Leave for 15 minutes to dissolve.

2 Stir in the egg yolk, salt, and 225 g/ 8 oz/2 cups of the flour. Add 115 g/ 4 oz/1 cup of the remaining flour and stir to make a soft dough.

3 Transfer to a floured surface and knead, adding flour if necessary, until the mixture is smooth and elastic. Place in a bowl, cover and leave to prove for 1½–2 hours.

4 Grease a baking sheet. Knock back the dough and cut it into 12 pieces, each the size of a golf ball.

5 Roll each piece into a rope shape, twist to form a knot and place the knots 2.5 cm/1 in apart on the baking sheet. Cover loosely and leave to prove for 1–1½ hours.

COOK'S TIP: Poppy seeds make an excellent topping for a range of rolls and breads. They look very attractive on plaited loaves, for example.

6 Preheat the oven to 180°C/350°F/ Gas 4. Brush the knots with the egg glaze and sprinkle over the poppy seeds. Bake for 25–30 minutes, until the tops are lightly browned. Cool slightly on a rack before serving.

Croissants

Served with homemade preserves, these melt-in-the-mouth, crescent-shaped rolls are the ultimate luxury for breakfast.

Makes 18

INGREDIENTS
500 g/1¼ lb/5 cups plain flour
7.5 ml/1½ tsp salt
10 ml/2 tsp caster sugar
15 ml/1 tbsp easy-blend dried yeast
325 ml/11 fl oz/1⅓ cups
     lukewarm milk
225 g/8 oz/1 cup butter, chilled
1 egg, beaten with 10 ml/2 tsp water,
     for glazing

1 Mix the flour, salt, sugar and yeast in a large bowl. Make a well in the centre and add enough of the milk to make a soft dough. Transfer to a clean bowl, cover and leave to prove for about 1½ hours.

2 Knead the dough until smooth. Wrap in greaseproof paper and chill for 15 minutes. Meanwhile, divide the butter in half and roll each half between two sheets of greaseproof paper to form a 15 x 10 cm/6 x 4 in rectangle.

3 On a floured surface, roll out the dough to a 30 x 20 cm/12 x 8 in rectangle. Place a sheet of butter in the centre. Fold the bottom third of dough over the butter, press to seal, then place the remaining butter sheet on top. Fold over the top third.

4 Turn the dough so the short side faces you. Roll it gently to a 30 x 20 cm/12 x 8 in rectangle. Fold in thirds as before, then wrap and chill for 30 minutes. Repeat this process twice more, then wrap and chill for at least 2 hours, or overnight.

5 Roll out the chilled dough to a thin rectangle, about 33 cm/13 in wide. Cut in half, then into triangles, 15 cm/6 in high, with a 10 cm/4 in base. Roll the triangles slightly to stretch them, then roll up from base to point. Place on baking sheets, curving to make crescents. Cover and leave to prove for 1–1½ hours.

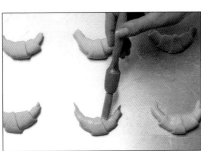

6 Preheat the oven to 240°C/475°F/ Gas 9. Brush the croissants with the egg glaze and bake for 2 minutes. Lower the oven temperature to 190°C/375°F/Gas 5 and bake for 10–12 minutes more, until golden. Serve warm.

Brioche

Rich and buttery, yet light and airy, this wonderful loaf captures the essence of the classic French bread.

Makes 1 loaf

INGREDIENTS
350 g/12 oz/3 cups unbleached white
    bread flour
2.5 ml/½ tsp salt
15 g/½ oz fresh yeast
60 ml/4 tbsp lukewarm milk
3 eggs
175 g/6 oz/¾ cup butter, softened
25 g/1 oz/2 tbsp caster sugar

FOR THE GLAZE
1 egg yolk
15 ml/1 tbsp milk

1 Sift the flour and salt into a large bowl and make a well in the centre. Stir together the yeast and milk. Add the yeast mixture to the well in the flour mixture with the eggs and mix together to form a soft dough.

2 Using your hand, beat the dough for 4–5 minutes until smooth and elastic. Cream the butter and sugar together. Gradually add the butter mixture to the dough in small amounts, making sure each amount is incorporated before adding more. Beat until smooth, shiny and elastic, then cover the bowl and leave to prove for 1–2 hours.

3 Lightly knock back the dough, then cover and place in the fridge for 8–10 hours or overnight.

4 Lightly grease a 1.6 litre/2¾ pint/ scant 7 cup brioche mould. Turn the dough out on to a lightly floured surface. Cut off almost a quarter, shape the rest into a ball and place in the mould. Shape the reserved dough into an elongated egg shape. Using two or three fingers, make a hole in the centre of the large ball of dough. Gently press the narrow end of the egg-shaped dough into the hole.

5 Mix together the egg yolk and milk for the glaze and brush a little over the brioche. Cover and leave to prove for 1½–2 hours.

6 Meanwhile, preheat the oven to 230°C/450°F/Gas 8. Brush the brioche with the remaining glaze and bake for 10 minutes. Reduce the oven temperature to 190°C/375°F/Gas 5 and bake for a further 20–25 minutes, or until golden. Turn out on to a wire rack to cool.

Plaited Loaf

This loaf, called *challah,* is a traditional Jewish egg bread that is served on the Sabbath and festive occasions.

Makes 1 loaf

INGREDIENTS
1 sachet easy-blend dried yeast
5 ml/1 tsp clear honey
250 ml/8 fl oz/1 cup lukewarm milk
50 g/2 oz/4 tbsp butter, melted
350 g/12 oz/3 cups plain flour
5 ml/1 tsp salt
1 egg, lightly beaten
1 egg yolk beaten with 5 ml/1 tsp milk,
    for glazing

1 Combine the yeast, honey, milk and butter, stir and leave for 15 minutes to dissolve.

2 In a large bowl, mix together the flour and salt. Make a well in the centre and add the yeast mixture and egg. Stir to make a rough dough.

3 Transfer to a floured surface and knead until smooth and elastic. Place in a clean bowl, cover and leave to prove for about 1½ hours.

4 Grease a baking sheet. Knock back the dough and divide into three equal pieces. Roll to shape each piece into a long thin strip.

5 Begin plaiting from the centre strip, tucking in the ends. Cover loosely and leave to prove for 30 minutes.

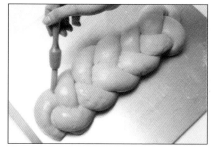

6 Preheat the oven to 190°C/375°F/ Gas 5. Place the bread in a cool place while the oven heats. Brush with the glaze and bake for 40–45 minutes, until golden. Cool on a rack.

Greek Easter Bread

Traditionally decorated with red-dyed eggs, this bread is made by bakers and in homes throughout Greece at Easter.

Makes 1 loaf

INGREDIENTS
25 g/1 oz fresh yeast
15–30 ml/1–2 tbsp lukewarm water
120 ml/4 fl oz/½ cup lukewarm milk
675 g/1½ lb/6 cups strong plain flour
2 eggs, beaten
2.5 ml/½ tsp caraway seeds
15 ml/1 tbsp caster sugar
15 ml/1 tbsp brandy
50 g/2 oz/4 tbsp butter, melted
1 egg white, beaten
50 g/2 oz/½ cup split almonds

FOR THE EGGS
3 eggs
1.5 ml/¼ tsp bright red food
  colouring paste
15 ml/1 tbsp white wine vinegar
5 ml/1 tsp water
5 ml/1 tsp olive oil

1 First make the egg decoration. Place the eggs in a pan of water and bring to the boil. Allow to boil gently for 10 minutes.

2 Meanwhile, mix the red food colouring, vinegar, water and olive oil in a shallow bowl. Remove the eggs from the pan, place on a wire rack for a few seconds to dry, then roll in the colouring mixture. Return to the rack to cool and dry.

3 Crumble the yeast into a bowl. Mix with the water until softened. Add the milk and 115 g/4 oz/1 cup of the flour and mix to a creamy consistency. Cover and leave in a warm place for 1 hour.

4 Sift the remaining flour into a large bowl and make a well in the centre. Pour the yeast mixture into the well and draw in a little of the flour from the sides. Add the eggs, caraway seeds, sugar and brandy. Incorporate the remaining flour, until the mixture begins to form a dough.

5 Mix in the melted butter. Turn the dough on to a floured surface and knead for about 10 minutes, until smooth. Return to the bowl, cover and leave to prove for 3 hours.

6 Preheat the oven to 180°C/350°F/ Gas 4. Knock back the dough, turn on to a floured surface and knead for 2 minutes.

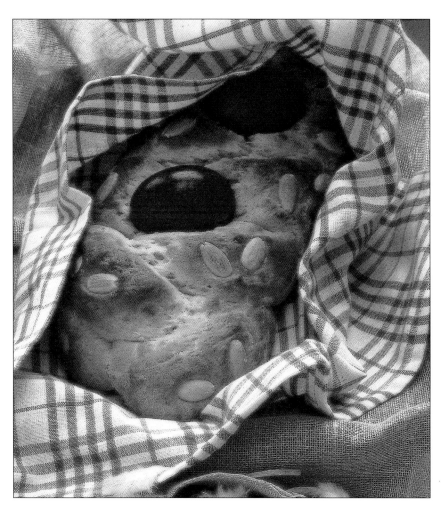

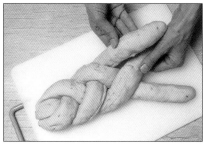

7 Divide the dough into three pieces and roll each piece into a long sausage shape. Make a plait and place the loaf on a greased baking sheet.

8 Tuck the ends under, brush with the egg white and decorate with the eggs and split almonds. Bake for about 1 hour. Cool on a wire rack.

Twelfth Night Bread

The traditional version of this Spanish bread contains a dried bean hidden inside – the lucky recipient is declared the king of the festival!

Makes 1 loaf

INGREDIENTS
450 g/1 lb/4 cups unbleached white
  bread flour
2.5 ml/½ tsp salt
25 g/1 oz fresh yeast
140 ml/scant ¼ pint/scant ⅔ cup mixed
  lukewarm milk and water
75 g/3 oz/6 tbsp butter
75 g/3 oz/6 tbsp caster sugar
10 ml/2 tsp finely grated lemon rind
10 ml/2 tsp finely grated orange rind
2 eggs
15 ml/1 tbsp brandy
15 ml/1 tbsp orange flower water
dried bean (optional)
1 egg white, lightly beaten, for glazing

FOR THE DECORATION
a mixture of candied and glacé fruit slices
flaked almonds

1 Lightly grease a large baking sheet. Sift the flour and salt into a large bowl. Make a well in the centre.

2 In a bowl, mix the yeast with the milk and water until the yeast has dissolved. Pour into the well and stir in enough of the flour to make a thick batter. Sprinkle a little of the remaining flour over the top of the batter and leave to sponge, in a warm place, for about 15 minutes, or until frothy.

3 Beat the butter and sugar together in a bowl until soft and creamy, then set aside.

4 Add the citrus rinds, eggs, brandy and orange flower water to the flour mixture and use a wooden spoon to mix to a sticky dough.

5 Using one hand, beat the mixture until it forms a fairly smooth dough. Gradually beat in the reserved butter mixture and beat for a few minutes until the dough is smooth and elastic. Cover and leave to prove for about 1½ hours.

6 Knock back the dough and turn out on to a lightly floured surface. Gently knead for 2–3 minutes, incorporating the lucky bean, if using. Using a rolling pin, roll out the dough into a long strip measuring about 65 x 13 cm/26 x 5 in.

7 Roll up the dough from one long side like a Swiss roll to make a long sausage shape. Place seam side down on the prepared baking sheet and seal the ends together. Cover and leave to prove for 1–1½ hours.

8 Meanwhile, preheat the oven to 180°C/350°F/Gas 4. Brush the dough ring with lightly beaten egg white and decorate with candied and glacé fruit slices, pushing them slightly into the dough. Sprinkle with almond flakes and bake for 30–35 minutes, or until risen and golden. Cool on a wire rack.

This edition is published by Southwater

Distributed in the UK by
The Manning Partnership,
251–253 London Road East, Batheaston,
Bath BA1 7RL, UK
tel. (0044) 01225 852 727
fax (0044) 01225 852 852

Distributed in Australia by
Sandstone Publishing,
Unit 1, 360 Norton Street, Leichhardt,
New South Wales 2040, Australia
tel. (0061) 2 9560 7888
fax (0061) 2 9560 7488

Distributed in New Zealand by
Five Mile Press NZ,
PO Box 33–1071, Takapuna,
Auckland 9, New Zealand
tel. (0064) 9 4444 144
fax (0064) 9 4444 518

Southwater is an imprint of Anness Publishing Limited

© 2000 Anness Publishing Limited

Publisher: Joanna Lorenz
Editor: Valerie Ferguson
Series Designer: Bobbie Colgate Stone
Designer: Andrew Heath
Editorial Reader: Marion Wilson
Production Controller: Joanna King

Recipes contributed by: Angela Boggiano,
Roz Denny, Nicola Graimes, Carole Handslip,
Christine Ingram, Patricia Lousada, Lesley Mackley,
Sallie Morris, Jennie Shapter, Liz Trigg, Jeni Wright.

Photography: William Adams-Lingwood,
Mickie Dowey, Joanna Farrow, Michelle Garrett,
John Heseltine, Amanda Heywood,
Janine Hosegood, Thomas Odulate.

1 3 5 7 9 10 8 6 4 2

Notes:
For all recipes, quantities are given in both metric and imperial measures and, where appropriate, measures are also given in standard cups and spoons.
Follow one set, but not a mixture, because they are not interchangeable.

Standard spoon and cup measures are level.

1 tsp = 5 ml   1 tbsp = 15 ml

1 cup = 250 ml/8 fl oz

Australian standard tablespoons are 20 ml. Australian readers should use 3 tsp in place of 1 tbsp for measuring small quantities of gelatine, cornflour, salt etc.

Medium eggs are used unless otherwise stated.

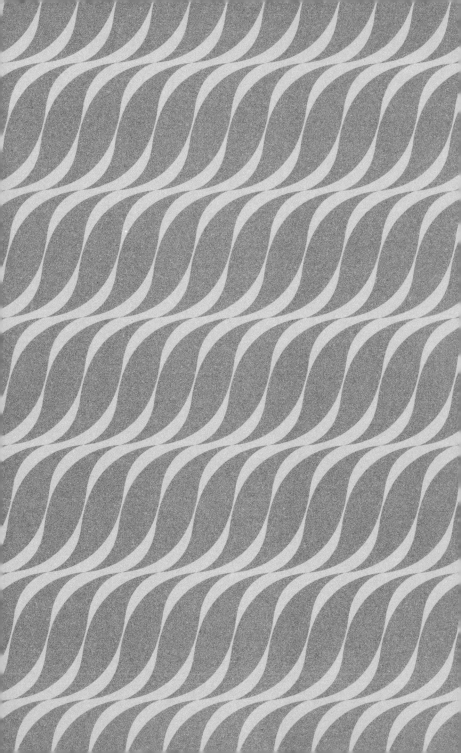